Young Learner's

Look-n-Colour FLOWERS

COSMOS

BLUE BELLS

HIBISCUS

TULIP

JASMINE

ROSE

SUNFLOWER

LILY

PHLOX

PEONY

DAFFODIL

LOTUS

MORNING GLORY

ALLAMANDA

POPPY

PANSY

DAHLIA

DAISY

ASTER

PRIMROSE

ZINNIA

CARNATION

MARIGOLD

PETUNIA

ORCHID

DANDELION

BIRDS OF PARADISE

PERIWINKLE

ANEMONE

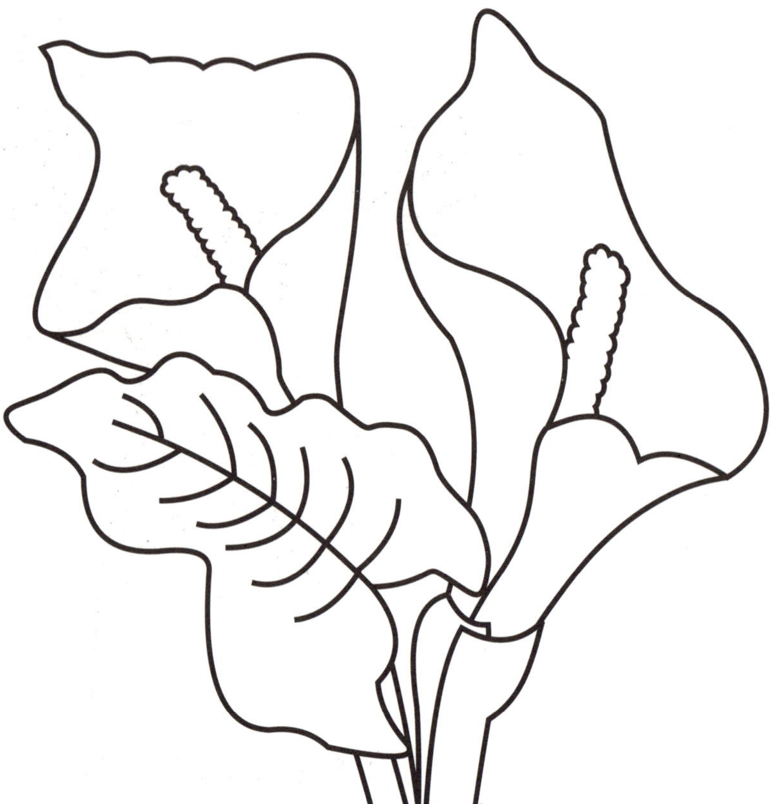

CALLA LILY

AMARYLLIS

PLUMERIA

COCKSCOMB

BUTTERCUP

CANNA

LAVENDER

GLADIOLUS

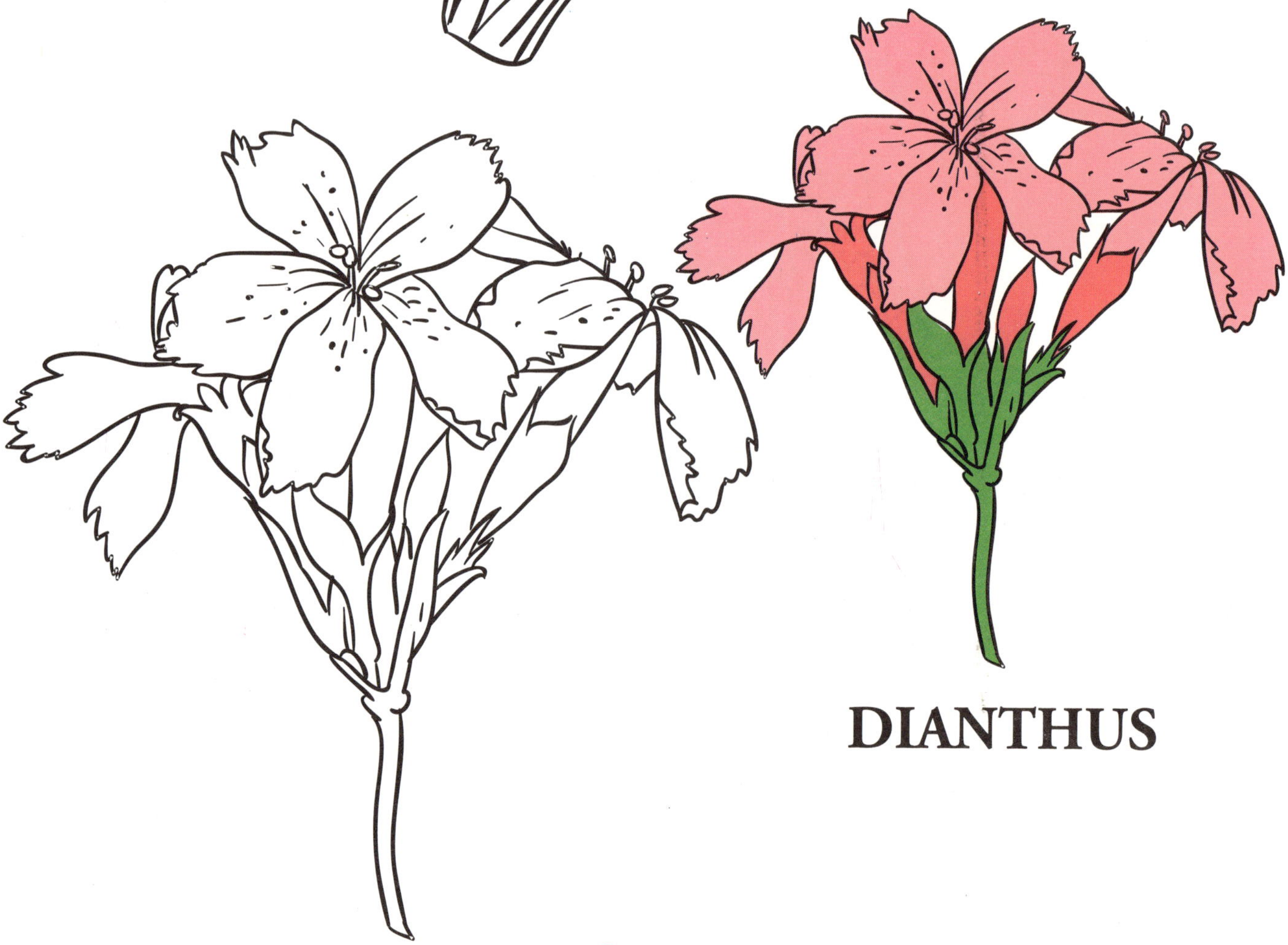

DIANTHUS

AFRICAN DAISY

BLANKET FLOWER

BEGONIA

BARREN STRAWBERRY

IRIS

PURPLE NARCISSUS

BIDENS

CONE FLOWER